WITHDRAWN

MY BROTHER GLOUCESTER

new poems

Michael Schmidt

DUFOUR EDITIONS, INC.

Acknowledgements are due to the editors of the following publications in which some of these poems first appeared: *Poetry* (USA), *Listener*, *Southern Review* (USA), *New Statesman*, *Hudson Review* (USA), *Antaeus*, *Caret*, *Poetry Nation*, *Critical Quarterly*, *Scotsman*, the 1973 *PEN Anthology*, and the 1974 *PEN Anthology*. 'The Fool' was commissioned by the Globe Playhouse Trust for the 1973 Shakespeare birthday anthology. Three of these poems were broadcast on 'Poetry Now' (BBC). 'Wasps Nest' appeared in *Young Winter's Tales 6* (Macmillan London Ltd., 1975).

Note

The title of this collection records my debt for marine imagery to Clarence's dream in *Richard III*. The poems subtitled 'after Pasternak' and 'after Hofmannsthal' were written from memory, without reference back to the original text, and should not be read as translations.

The following poems carry specific dedications: 'The Judas Fish' is for Nora and Charles Sisson, 'The Cure' is for Elizabeth Jennings, 'Writing' is for Betty Hill Storke, 'Words' is for Matthew Schmidt, 'My Town' is for Renee and Alan Young, 'The City of the Dead' is for Jean and Brian Cox, 'The Fool' is for Aileen and Robert Nye, 'Sea Currency' is for Jeanne O'Brien, 'Conjuring' is for Val Warner, 'The Totem' is for Doreen and Donald Davie, 'The English Lesson' is for Alexandra Seddon, 'Litter' is for Priscilla and Roger Garfitt, 'The Figure' is for Robert B. Shaw, 'The Shells' is for Brenda and Charles Tomlinson, 'The Freeze' is for Peter Jones, 'The Diving Bell' is for Marilyn and John Schmidt, and 'The Sleigh' is for Carole and Gareth Reeves.

The book is dedicated to the memory of
    Mary Louise Seaver 1890-1974
    Carl Bernhardt Schmidt 1892-1970
    John MacAllister 1909-1974

Copyright © 1976 Michael Schmidt

LCC No. 75-43116
SBN 8023 1255 1

First published in the United States 1976
by Dufour Editions, Inc.
Chester Springs
Pennsylvania 19425

Printed in Great Britain
by W & J Mackay Limited, Chatham
by photo-litho

CONTENTS

THE FABLES I

THE JUDAS FISH

I wake to this bewilderment —
my porthole's gone under, the sea flows
too high tonight, and trickles in.
It is not rain, but wind that lifts
and leaves it hovering.

Moments pass without the sky at all.
I share the water-dark that is a sound
intimately chilling, like a voice that whispers
from the world a charm into a dream.
Through the latched porthole

the gentle bleeding from the sea
will be tomorrow a salt web across the floor.
I light my lamp against the starless voice.
It is my face that looks me in the eye.
I cup my hands, look closer

through the face into a shallow pool of light.
A fish might take the porthole for a mild
luminous fish-eye; a night diver
might spot it from a distance as a coin,
antique, the frail imperial face

on alloyed gold, wide-eyed,
not negotiable, gazing
into the marches around empire
where froth is the untouchable barbarian.
Looking out, indeed, there is not much to see,

no diver, no near fish, nothing
to crave possession over,
though there is a strange
possessiveness in water, as in sunlight,
determining the shadows. Water casts up

shadows of a curious kind, swirling
three inches from the eyes — an impulse
to undo the latch for once, gingerly
to invite oblivion in,
let the driving current touch and have its way.

Yet it is a driven current at the pane
that has claimed as many histories as time
and planted them in beds of sand and coral,
in thicket weeds, in feeding of its fish;
its fluid memory retains suspended

elements of mountains, ships and mariners
unredeemable as salt within the blood,
but present: the dead are tasted
like rich sediment, flooding
the secret latitudes.

Subsiding with the wind the water goes,
my porthole fills with constellations
that never touched a life,
and they are welcome, identifiable —
although before they came back I believe

a fish pulsed into view in the dwindling water
with thirty silver scales upon its side
and a Judas eye trained on me, focusing.
I slipped the latch then.
It was starlight that came in.

THE CURE

The physician is visiting
the tree the squirrels inhabit.
It is Autumn. The tree in breeze
feeds its giant cavity with leaves.
Perhaps the squirrels have bedded down.

Like a surgeon at a sickbed
this man carries tools.
He rolls his sleeve
up to the knotty elbow, reaches in.
He moves his hand inside the hollow tree.

I have felt within the tree as well.
It is a long way down and strangely warm.
The sides are rough, with little pits of moss.
The bottom has a fur I thought was animal.
It is a nest, and there are corridors

deeper and narrower you cannot reach,
noiseless, secure as catacombs:
cobweb and leafmould and the squirrels' harvest.
The squirrels are in there —
once I was bitten.

The man looks in with a torch.
What colours does a hole as dark as that
yield, deep in the faulted heart of growth?
Browns and mossy shades, or like a sick man's heart
a dwindling crimson, the pale blue veins?

In handfuls he pulls out
the moss that felt like fur.
He sprays a chemical into the hole.
He carries bricks and mortar from his car.
Row on row the cavity is sealed.

For years it's been the squirrels' sanctuary —
nest and silos and their granaries —
where no sound came and cold was moderate.
Now the air's stanched out,
the tree is healed

ostensibly. Immured,
the sleepers will be skeletons
before they're met again. There are effects
we do not live to see, cold destinations
we have observed so quietly, we caused them.

WRITING

The cone-snail shrinks from us.
Its mouth is sealed.
Nothing will tempt it out again
but washing in the sea. It is cast up.
We gather it with shells and take it home.

Of all that we collected it is this
we look at first. It's edged with tiny stings.
We set it on the floor
and bring the reading glass to make it large.
It leaks a yellow liquid like a wound.

In the lip there is a rim of glyphs.
They are crimson on pearl white, each
distinctly written, like a text we magnify.
These tendril lines are veins
that bear poison to the stings.

If we knew how to read
we could not deny a language here.
The fluent tracery is more
than a snail articulating vanity:
it is a charm to keep its body whole.

An eyeless thing
fingering with blunt horns
the walls it grew, gradually
sketched these images,
translating them by instinct into shell;

it was a jelly substance working sand,
fitting itself to sand and sand to it,
observing the reciprocal slow laws
to make its long vault issue from the heart
up to the lips and there describe these symbols.

We cannot pry open the fixed mouth.
Does the writing continue in the throat,
through the length of the deep whorl, until
at the core the riddle is resolved?
We tap it. It fractures like egg-shell.

In the innermost recess the snail has shrivelled
hard as a pea. We are deceived:
the vaults are white throughout,
and what there was to say was clearly
written on the lips and spoken there.

WORDS
(after Hofmannsthal)

Child, your eyes will darken soon with wonder —
and darken ignorantly till they're blind.
We will pass by you as we were passed by.

The fruit is bitter. It will sweeten in the dark
and drop into your hands with broken wings.
Cherish it a day. But it will die.

The wind comes down to you from history.
It chilled us too. The phrases it repeats
are stale with pleasure, stale with punishment.

The paths lead from the garden to the world,
to places where light burns among the trees
that raise their wings but cannot hope to fly.

Who cast the root of everything so deep
that nothing flies away that we can name?
Why can we laugh and in a moment cry

and give a name to laughter and to tears?
What is the illness that our eyes grow dark?
—We are men because we are alone:

we touch and speak, but silence follows words
the way a shadow does, the hand draws back.
The curtain blows and there is no one there.

What removed you to this solitude,
into this common light, this common twilight?
It is that word, twilight, that called you down —

a word the wind has handed on to us
undeciphered, and it might be love —
rich with a honey pressed from hollow combs.

THE GHOSTS

MY TOWN

It is as though the whole town is on ice.
Skaters with a speed of birds
greet each other on reflected cloud
mid-stream, up-stream, past the crippled boats.
There is a horse and sledge.
A bonfire burns its censer shape into the cold.
Someone sells grilled fish

again today, for it's been weeks
the river froze, and a man dared
walk out on the water.
No one has looked back since:
ice-fishermen with saw and string,
the schools of children, the slower
shopkeepers like large sedate fish.

The habitual town has ceased. It's chosen
another better world, a world of days
prayed for, persistent beyond hope,
a flowering of impossibilities.
Buildings line the shore
derelict like plundered sea-chests
and the pirate is the ice.

I tie on my skates and find the air
moves me like a feather from the shore.
I leave town for the frozen falls.
I fly up-stream like a salmon, light
with spawn. I come home
and pass by for the sea, and turn again.
Sun sparks my blades, I send up

grit of ice like quick flame.
I burn my hours religiously,
my ceremony to the ice and air.

But today the air is warmer, our days
are numbered. The falls are dripping
and the sea barks and barks
into the brittle river mouth. It is like

sailing at the end of a brief world, beyond
responsibility, and time is purposeless,
pure of daily history and bread.
To put on wings is an authentic dream, and yet
up on shore the dirtied nest of facts
is patient in the sun, tall and lowering
above the vistas of the heart,

and even now beneath the ice
the other world continues
undisturbed, the weeds are spun by currents,
the pearls increase to buy our future eyes;
the small fish feed, are fed on, the great
round-eyed flounder old as water
subsist on certainties among stilled keels
and out to sea, by rough boulders and the light,
the wrecked laden hulls, the mariners . . .

If the inhabitants of that world look up
they perceive hairline cracks
fissuring the ice
and our veined shadows pass
against the light like baits
they will not take, but wait —
cold acolytes, whose business is
each candle and the dark.

THE CITY OF THE DEAD
(the cemetery at Parana)

We could not come at night.
The gates are locked. Besides,
the dead may walk about, whatever we believe.
Today is safe and hot.
There are no people here.

It is a city built for dwarfs —
or are the dead reduced
to dolls in grieving minds?
For in each edifice
a coffin is the heart.

We come to see, not the dead, but how
the dying longed for tangible rewards.
Relations bought off grief
by building the final wish in stone.
So the weaver has his shop — inside,

a tiny loom. The sexton earns a church
where he performs the office.
The barren woman keeps
a mansion her longing would have filled.
She is a mother here.

But in each edifice
a coffin is the heart.
It is a baroque city, with cornices
and tracery, cupolas and bells,
elbow-high; it is like toys

contrived for a still-born child.
Here is a stone effigy.
She gathers up her gown
but it is snared by thistles.
She gazed once on a grave

that is become wild garden.
She is like a child.
From windows round about
carved faces frown if someone comes to mourn.
Death is so selfish — or the living are

who plan their future in the stunted world.
The streets are cleaner here
than our habitual streets.
The dead are tidier.
The living see to that.

These, then, are their hopes —
comfortable, pacific.
This is the city they would build in heaven
using the moon for tavern light,
the stars as currency, and God

would have his church there as on earth,
although he might sometimes
explore the avenues
and talk with traders in the square like Christ.
— But faith cannot raise stones

into the sky above the yellow grass.
To be interred beneath a wish
confines the soul to bones,
and in each edifice
a coffin is the heart.

We go unnoticed here.
We are not of this world —
like living men who pass down Hell's
long corridors, and brush
with shadows only the agonies that wait.

THE FOOL

I warn you, said the Fool,
I have a job to do. I do it well.
I am the lowest rung on the man ladder;
my place, unchallenged, is not inconvenient

for I look up and undersee your polished boots
holed through utterly beneath, your hosiery
tattered at the knee, and you in silks outside
below are bare as apricots, as radishes.

Your bodies' downward scent is unperfumed.
I smell your misdemeanours and your motives.
— Yet every heart beats only from my heart
if it beats truly, though no voice speaks

my language. None speaks truly.
In my rhetoric I am in the earth the undertaker,
the first worm who bears the licensed key
and unlocks every body: mine

is the first taste, my certificate
implies a corpse impure enough to plunder.
I am the deepest, oldest, thinnest fish
upon the seabed in the rocks and sand:

I see the world entire in glancing up,
I intercept and touch the whale's long sound,
the prim sea-horse I watch grow old and faithless,
the sallow bladder-fish inflate and fawn

on sleek sea-kale trees that stand up like kings.
And yet I have no name but my two eyes,
my speech that none replies to,
a venerable, antique uniform.

I have — I'm had on sufferance.
I am afraid of dark as much as you.
I pull my cap across my eyes and sleep.
I dream of an ignorant and sunny kingdom

trivial, passionate, where all have hearts
within undisfigured bodies that are breathing
like men and women coming out of marble
into an actual day, as fish move out from weeds

blinking at the galleons that sink
and break before them on the seabed, spilling
treasure meaningless and brilliant, habitable;
and the drowned mariners more slowly drifting
touch down as gently dead as leaves.

STANDING IN HIS CHURCHYARD
(for Edwin Muir)

Your shield was decorative and impotent,
the horses that rode on it — cart horses.
What could it do against the spectral hounds,
whirlwinds — against the grey stone later,
the brick that spawned a little black moss
precious, rare as northern ebony?

Your history held you
as a furrow holds a plough,
and looking back the immediate earth
writhed serpent-like,
but settled to dead clay
far off, rearranged.

The serpents died in time, as they will do;
and yet you moved on unsafe till you turned
serpents and the city like the shield,
and nothing immanent but all things
distanced, pared down to fit
a legend, repainted

on frail mats. Once you climbed a hill
and looked on Tintern.
Severing it from the generous
context of bracken
you reset the granite ribs
on Troy plain where the wind

blows only cold, and colder
on ash that will not glow. Wily,
without vision of sufficiency,
you walked home over the green sea
ten years to comfort.
Rust moves on the shield,

mottling the thick horses to abstracts;
the bells that cannot ring to you
are ringing, their iron petals
shed on those familiar hills
that make no skyline,
that are literal graves.

SEA CURRENCY

The tide goes and lets them out again.
Circles in the sand like tiny coins
minted of colourless shell-alloy
rise by a delicate instinct, as by air,
and out the frailest ivory spiders —
bone chips with legs of whisker — come
trace their imperceptible footprints.

At low tide in hundreds they emerge
into a town of faceless citizens,
their homes identical, their natures unsociable,
secretive. Because they have no life
but leaving home and coming home,
because they're legion as hairs upon a head,
we're attracted to their anonymity.

We sit still as weeds.
They sense we are not there.
Each hunts the stranded plankton.
Some advance on us zig-zag
like actual spiders, perceive abruptly
that we breathe and gaze — they scurry home,
draw down their hatches tight
as though our breathing blew them out.

They are the ghosts of spiders.
They have tombs.
Their history goes back to the first tides,
two chronicles, of daily drowning and of air.
They cannot swim,
they have no wings to fly.
An early wave would take them or the wind
if of their eight feet they put one foot wrong —
weightless misers with their coins drawn
watertight upon impermeable abodes.

Those coins won't prise up
but fragment to thin laths of sand like mica.
Underneath, when you have broken in,
nothing exists but the white, minute
life-chalice, like a cartridge, the spider
not at home, though we have seen it
enter at the door and batten down.

Mightier, more regular across the sand
than us, at evening the tide.
We and the insect-eating birds
are moved up-beach, water hushes
over talon- and foot-print.
The tombs, the homes that are unbroken
leave us, entering their other element,
the ghosts within commence the life of waiting:

the spiders lie in like living pearls
and generate their oyster out of darkness,
or I think they rest like tongues in mouths,
stilled, and bear upon their lips the obolus
to bribe the boatman who has never come.

STAINS
(Naples)

I know they're ghosts.
There in the vestry where they take the toll
I handed in my hat.
Others were by me in the passageway
and here they watch, grown huge,

humpbacks and a faceless girl
whose body oozes from the surface world
in stringy rivulets on to the stones.
I have a coin for her.
I only stepped inside because it rained.

They're damp rising from graves trodden nameless.
The fresco martyrdoms are flaked and gone
to leprous ghosts that overtake
the tracery, the Stations of the Cross.
Ascetics out of the way but watchful,

they may prove cruel and rot the altar's house
or contrive penances we shall enact.
Their stealth is thinking: we will know their time;
flames of votive stars play over them
and gutter. They're increased:

oblivion draws them out,
jaundiced, sexless, gathering
taller into angels — powers
of the cold house: impermanence.
Their sexton eyes me with his one good eye.

He'll be a ghost on these walls too,
even his ring of keys
to each dark passage and the stony heart —
confessor of forbidden darknesses.
I will not cross his palm.

I will abide
before the candles at the Virgin's skirt,
offering as wicks do blackened silence,
numbering tokens of the prayers yes answered:
tiny silver hearts, a curling rose;

these are the poverty of given things.
The stains suck tears from air and rise
gentle as shadows till they touch the vault.
They hang there, inquisitors, not breathing.
Nowhere to go, they give themselves to us,

devising trials for those who do not know.
How old are they? Job's heart
was flayed, although he could not die;
and Greco knew them as the spike of light
splitting the saint's eye; and Galileo, too,

proscribed, because he saw beyond the vault
spheres circling in a silence more than prayer,
forgot the rosary and rote, instead
clutching a white diamond eye,
patient for darkness and their planted stars.

CONJURING

We wait the ghost.
The air has been prepared.
There is a candle, otherwise the dark.
No draught can enter. Grip me by the hand.
It makes us nervous for we half-believe.

How close the silence is. The one you chose
of all the dead, who knows, may come —
another may. The door is bolted.
Whatever happens must be less than air,
move in the wick, a spark, a flickering.

How was it done before? And done, did they
let go the dead and move away unaltered?
Will we give credit like the alchemist
who more than raising gold out of base ore
was faithful to the tense uncertainty,

acolyte to embers and the crucible?
If nothing comes, no doubt
we'll pester death again, flirting half-hearted
with a faith that history's forsaken.
When no one called on them the spirits rose

and touched and lay beside you in the night;
there was a world unquestionable, unknown,
that hinted at itself and might be won —
but gently, by slow faith
that did not quiver when the candle spoke.

We turn inwards to the quality of sleep
to find the dead in us —
not our own slow fossils,
the lost girl, lost boy,
but what we were before we disbelieved.

There are sharp tools at work against the flame.
They fillet it, and then the dark
enters us like cold upon the quick.
It is your hand, my hand. We clutch the loss.
The ghost is here between us like a fist.

THE WARDER
(for Delmore Schwartz)

Pluto's, Plato's, whose cave? My cave
crawling with the downhill lights of cars
and alternately greying, brightening,
those years of false days following the same
decline to different lives like animals,
roll up the dark then let the dark drop down.

Forms fall against the wall, thin prisoners
thrown in and forced until they scale and shrivel.
When the curtain blows they dance.
No two are similar.
They do not touch or merge
but singly rise and swerve.

If they behaved like sheep
I could count flocks and sleep.
I have no libation to pour out
and find if they are ghosts
or merely Plato's forms.
By the roots I draw the bedclothes up

burying my face. The darkness is a choice.
I hear outside the voices
of the inner lights switch gear,
descending to a common quietness.
I try to force the old door made of horn.
My key won't fit. The lock's been changed.

I lie. Here are the bones of light
in chains. They move descriptively —
I do not move.
Now the air
sucks the wardrobe open. Those lightnesses
slide in. They're trying on my clothes,

entering one by one and staying there.
There is still room;
there is no end of room.
Night on night we will not see the end.
I take in these substitutes,
the animals I keep.

THE CRYPT

The crypt goes deep
as wells would have to do
in poorer lands. It underlies
the market-gardens like a tuber,
rootless, set out in the wrong season.

It veins beneath the town as well
with its alternative — the shadow
avenues, the final houses
no one has to do up any more, unswept,
unhaunted by births or marriages.

Tenants hang out
no laundry but epitaphs.
They move through time in a cold
idleness, as the broken snail
drags on its altered pain.

No sound comes here but,
hurried by a lamp, footsteps
to witness emptiness for a gratuity
and take the sight of nothing home
memento-like, to turn at leisure

into whatever it will be.
That nothing is light to pack,
simple to smuggle back
to places ignorant of the unseeded night
in which dark hangs like flannel —

its touch perfecting
a current isolation.
Moving underground, we look up
as though through muddy water at the mud.
Feeling for growth this deep

we find sharp crippled blooms of limestone,
and the pale-fingered spiders move like hair
between the bedrooms of the dead.
The crypt resolves whatever ghosts we bring.
We surface to unportioned solitude.

THE TOTEM

Time left its marks in circles at the heart
beneath the bark, and one a year it gave —
anonymous, true charity — the rings

to the one natural tree in a blue forest.
Now that the conifers are cut for pulp,
their infinite cold regiments recalled

only by rows of stumps like standard tombs,
the last tree is alone, an oak
encompassing centuries of wood.

The branches have been lopped
and scattered with the tenants,
with nests that hung against the light

like mistletoe and held
the shells and feathers of the rooks.
Hard-eyed birds hop on crisp needles

and the paper leaves, or are circling.
Time is up, and history is here —
that other progress that is vertebrate

and speaks, subduing all things to the useful —
harvester. On the oak, in error,
in hacking off the branches it has made

not a clean trunk but a crude totem
for the saw, unveiled on the naked bark
faces of animals and men, a rough stump

with fingers and a stump with claws.
Slit by metal a wood-ant city spilled
its hoarded generation down the bark.

Insects stumble through the scar.
The wooden faces gaze
as though they were not wood,

the tree almost invisibly is bleeding
for the roots are ignorant and pump
what they can of earth into the shafts of air.

But history replaces weather and the seasons,
is closing an old wound and opening
another with new qualities of pain:

the green wood has its flame.
It lights within us
a suburb where integrities survive,

frail, unaccountable as instincts;
and though eyeless as eroded skulls
they recognize the totem as no mere chance:

it is intimate, an echo that we quell
in severing the ancient and the newer rings
to violate the heart as property.

THE ENGLISH LESSON
(after Pasternak)

When it was Desdemona's turn to sing
and only minutes of her life remained,
she did not mourn her star, that she had loved:
she sang about a tree, a willow tree.

When it was Desdemona's time to sing,
her voice grew deeper, darker as she sang;
the darkest, coldest demon kept for her
a weeping song of streams through rough beds flowing.

And when it was Ophelia's turn to sing
and only minutes of her life remained,
she was dry as light, as a twig of hay:
wind blew her from the loft into the storm.

And when it was Ophelia's time to sing,
her dreams were waning, all but the dream of death.
Bitter and tired — what tokens sank with her?
In her hair wild celandine, and willows in her arms.

Then letting fall the rags of human passion,
heart-first they plunged into the flowing dark,
fracturing their bodies like white tinder,
silencing their unbroken selves with stars.

THE SLEIGH
(after a theme of Turgenev)

The colours have gone out.
It is like death — blind white
and the sun is white: we speed
the way we always wished —
a sleigh, the harness bells — across the snow.

It's not what we expected.
Afraid on the ice road
we ring to the empty farms
that we've come their way but not to stop.
Who set the burning pennies on our eyes?

Think — if the runners struck a rut
and hurled us into temporary graves
face-down like heretics; or if the jingling
ceased and we flew silently
on into the open throat of night.

Speed and the snow
blend field and hedge and landmark
in one whiteness like a future.
Perhaps the thaw will turn it up like new —
and yet we cannot see that far today.

Under the arcane dunes
suppose the past is unreclaimable
too truly for March sun and its tired miracle.
What if a half-hearted wish for warmth
is all we bring ourselves, and bring no love

hot to melt the things it cannot love?
What if we trust all changes to the snow?
I think the snow will see us off:
we're going to die
whirling, two flakes

of headlong colour
over the unmarked brink.
In a flash of white, as though we are to hang,
we shall relive our separate short lives.
— We have not touched or taken

the feather weight of pain.
If it was war, then we were traitors there.
If it was famine, we ate on and on; and now
we're turned to cowards in a day we owned,
returned as serfs to fields we ruled as czars,

we plough the snow where once
we led the hunt through hedge and stream-bed
up to the lodge and there were ladies there.
It is neglect and snow leave open graves
we ride from to worry at a world

we partly chose, and where
forgetfulness makes easy graves we go
across a brilliance like purity
to no known place.
The driver turns and points but we are blind.

I dread a destination and the thaw
that will set us down and leave us to ourselves
as we are now. We are
the dying penitent who feels too late
the cold breath of the beggar on his hand.

I wish I could look on
rather than be here a piece of blindness.
I would not call
to those who go together
and seem upon the snow as cold as snow,

but from a distant cottage I would watch
a tiny horse advance
with a faint pulse of bells
drawing its burden, as a spider draws a fly
across its web of light into the dark.

NATALYA'S DREAM
(for N.E.Gorbanevskaya,
detained in prison mental hospital)

Her heart peers out
between her breathing shoulder-blades:
curious, fist-sized.

It gazes down the spine
as down a highway. From its high vantage
it observes unbroken snow,

the broken slumber, broken snow.
Under glacial contours of the skin
the lakes persist, dilate; the rivers

irrigate so deep cartographers ignore them.
Aya, Raya, her Estonian names
conjure their villages,

the farmers who received her
in their houses and their language:
how they are squinting,

blinded by their fields of snow,
how the one road leads
one way and loses them.

There, at the highway's end,
Tartu, a pole of exile.
Here, between the shoulders,

the other pole of exile is the heart —
renewing the old journeys
with each syllable of pulse —

until it flickers like a candle, votive,
ignited to the guardian of exiles,
shadowed out by the twin blades of bone.

She wakes to the ward smell
and sound of other dreaming,
in a frayed prison smock, in the early light;

to her face reflected from the dusty pane:
a face of Russia with no caption, with no
black border, no number and no name.

THE CREATURES

LOOKING FOR SNAKES

Dust trails lead off like veins into a stone.
The trails are recent, for a breeze
would take the traces into it.
The breeze has not moved and the dust is still.

We follow the dust trails to brittle grass.
The snakes that made these ways are all
the drought leaves motion to:
their thumb-thick directions veer at stones,

drawing like a charm on the dust surface
roots that this year have not taken.
The Indians make such pictures to cause rain.
In places the dust is dried so fine

the trails show scale marks where a serpent paused.
On a dead bush we find a token —
a sloughed skin, a mummy-fruit
with which a year was left behind entire.

What memory does a snake hang up,
painlessly departing from its skin
into the paths that end at entrances
hard-edged like thresholds, narrow,

deeply cool to touch? Digging,
we lose the way in stones. No doubt
it grows to damp cool corridors
in which a snake might pass for flowing water

down to chambers where our sound becomes
inconsequential language to the deaf
tenant who is soundlessly at home,
cold-blooded, but warm upon its nest,

in the earth as a bird is in the night,
or coiled root-like about its seed.

LITTER

Like eggs impatiently deserted,
the owl-pellets litter a rough nest —
perfect ovals pressed into the straw
by a heaviness of birds, as bulbs might be
set out in moss this time of year to wait.

The owls gave up the season
and emigrated, leaving their movables,
their straw and spoor, for the fortunate
next-comer. We climb to the high
hollow in the tree.

We look in.
Here there is down
and twigs like talons. And the owl
pellets, hard to the touch, scentless,
smooth as shells. A prick with a pen-knife

breaks the first globe, spilling
dust and a clutch of white we blow on
until it is the perfect skeleton
of a mouse curled up, clean as though
a natural death had washed it in the soil.

Another pellet gives up four small teeth
and the whole foot of a bird,
splayed as though standing on firm ground.
So it entered the body
of its predator and did

no damage; and the mouse seems
to have slept its process through,
intact as bone. What did it have to fear
once the talons ringed and lifted it —
a still, warm burden — home,

certain of the pilot and the port?
The beak that finally had it
was another burrow merely.
Featherlike it drifted to the pool
of acid and was drowned.

We have no use for it.
It clings to your knife,
a stiff twist of white hair,
a whisker — delicate
child of the night hunter, inanimate as pearl.

EXCUSES

I caught the fish but then
I could not kill it.
It sloughed and shivered rainbows.
It was the living crock of silver, mine
by a string. Treacherous purse. Erotic bird.

Finders keep what they weren't looking for;
but I can't slide my fingers down the line
over the brittle lips to smooth
the bladed sides. I lack
the healer's gesture in a killer's hand.

The thread entered the mouth. The wire
crooked in the throat. My throat closed.
Air is the same as pain;
the fish twists and flickers,
legless dancer. By mistake

I took the worm and put it on the point,
I cast and settled back for quiet.
Disquiet comes. It was not what I meant.
I did not really do it.
And if I did, how was I to know?

It was the fish chose finally, the fish
snatched the stiff worm and ran for it.
I let it go first but it took my line.
I couldn't stand for that.
I reeled it in.

— My lies are doors
into this narrow place.
It followed me. Is this
the first time I've lifted
something I cannot hold?

It hurts. If one comes as far as this
one ought to be considerate and kill.
But give it a little time, it will die:
killing's too hard when the thing
has eyes, is silver lost in an atmosphere

it used to kiss; is here out of a slow
gregarious element, quiet and threatless,
reciprocating tides; is torn
inside and cannot tell but sway
and tremble on the air like rain.

And it hangs still then.
Sun turns it warm.
My fingers find it and draw out the hook.
I do not want it. I toss it back —
pale belly up, a scar upon the heart.

THAW

The spider slept in ice a hundred days
and woke again
and crawled into the thaw
fresh on his eight fingers,
no hungrier, no older,

retaining still the secret
of the snow-flake web,
the ice sting and white sack
for witless bugs.
Why kill him then, as he hitches up

his elbows and tugs
free of the plated drain into full view?
Why not fish him out on a spoon and set him
spinning in the suburb of a last year's web?
And yet, because he moves

so unpredictably, like a severed hand
let loose within the sink, his browns
like rust or nicotine, his blacks
that have been playing
with darkness our drains mercifully conceal;

because he carries unaware
classified information
and might trail it any night
across the loaf, along the ceiling,
or find out sleep and pick

among the bristles of our dream,
infecting it, it is not viable
to keep him scampering, independent.
The ice preserved him. Heat
will take him off effectively.

A touch of boiling water and
he is a withered fist, a clot
of coffee grounds swilled into the thaw,
our memory almost
unafflicted, now the drains are free.

THE MOLE

The mole's at home in its perpetual curfew.
It has emerged at accidental doors and twitched
the scales from its eyes, confronting
a blur world of stems. It has confirmed
that it's for the dark and taken

again to its given certainties.
It has a stratum of the earth to mine.
It makes its passages of solitude,
the darkest ways desire could want
but never muster. Days are a rambling

edifice of corridors, a progress with no pomp
but sometimes the special taste of truffles.
Pushing its moraine about the lawn
it relandscapes my garden between flags
and juniper, then in a morning digs

under the fence, starts on the neighbour field,
withdrawing its lazy map into
low-profit country, building its long home
where no room is twice visited,
no thread reeled out for hindsight.

The lintels one by one come down in chambers
contrived like histories to be, once lived
and littered with invertebrate debris,
perpetually untenanted.
The mole evolves its labyrinth

until one unremarkable hot day
the farmer taps the furrow with his spade.
He digs the mole in two and leaves it covered.
It bleeds into the roots.
It will be bread.

IN THE AIR

It's a hunter's moon, red
as dead coral. Tonight we counted —
we lost count — of the hours.
The reeds have closed around the pool.
The pool has lost all record of our catch:

we brought home three trout
in shallow water, wondering
at the thirst they felt as air
began to stiffen them with little gulps
in the pail that sloshed to our pace.

By trailing hooks we lift them out,
silver as pale tubers, silver-green,
and slimed with tendril weeds.
As the gritty water lets them go
they feel the night along their swallow bodies,

their mouths become stiff ovals in the air.
You flap them flat on the ground.
Their painless eyes gaze on the scene of death:
this, then, is the air, and these its creatures;
here there is no grace in how things move,

and the dead do not float up
gently to the surface and lie still.
— You clean them with a knife.
You chafe the tiny coins into the pail.
You gut and lay them out beside their bones.

The eyes don't notice what they look upon.
We wear the silver, and the moon has found
a thousand burning mirrors on our wrists.
The scales stick. Our hands are fish in water
where they touch. We draw them up like roots.

THE FIGURE

Not like the bird
that strayed into Bede's vision
that he said as it turned
and disappeared through a high window
figured the life of man —
a sparrow after hours as I read to sleep
flapped in off the dark eaves
alarmed by an owl or an echo.
It flailed its shadow on my wall and face.
It figured nothing but a night-bird's fear.
I was afraid.

Not like Bede's bird,
its flight was intermittent.
It did not soar. It stuttered at the wall.
It did not perch and sing. It did not whistle.
It ricocheted and fell and tried again
and found no opening though the window opened.
Not like Bede's figure —
warm, its silly pulse still flickering,
I closed my hand around it.
I lifted it and laid it on the sill.
It did not sing then though its beak was open.

CAVE POOL

We pick the fish out with our torches,
the blind cave fish that move in a blind shoal,
fan out, contract, fan out,
like breathing of a single organism.
They eat algae off each other's scales,
the film that thickens in their vacant eyes.

Our light has touched them,
though their sockets do not register the glare.
Puce, intimate flesh-shades, crimson,
they are whiskerless sleek forms
with only translucent tissue fins
to pulse them through the dark.

They regroup, corpuscular on black,
responding to a beam
they have not felt in history;
dazed by the sensation, they waver
in an ordered rank, like birds on lines
expecting crumbs or lightning.

We have drawn a protean diagram
with our bright torches on the water —
until we're moved to speak,
and they, not frightened, but because the spell
breaks at the echo in the stone,
hardly flex their bodies and file out

as messengers with news of light and sound
into the earth. Our torches cannot follow:
one by one they pass down corridors
that vein beneath our feet, our continent,
to the darker heart that makes
pulse-echo of this penetrable dark.

WASPS' NEST

It was the fruit I wanted, not the nest.
The nest was hanging like the richest fruit
against the sun. I took the nest

and with it came the heart, and in my hand
the kingdom and the queen, frail surfaces,
rested for a moment. Then the drones

awoke and did their painful business.
I let the city drop upon the stones.
It split to its deep palaces and combs.

It bled the insect gold,
the pupa queens like tiny eyes
wriggled from their sockets, and somewhere

the monarch cowered in a veil of wings
in passages through which at evening
the labourers had homed,

burdened with silence and the garden scents.
The secret heart was broken suddenly.
I, to whom the knowledge had been given,

who was not after knowledge but a fruit,
remember how a knot of pains
swelled my hand to a round nest;

blood throbbed in the hurt veins
as if an unseen swarm mined there.
The nest oozed bitter honey.

I swaddled my fat hand in cotton.
After a week pain gave it back to me
scarred and weakened like a shrivelled skin.

A second fruit is growing on the tree.
Identical — the droning in the leaves.
It ripens. I have another hand.

THE FABLES II

OF ANGELS

What if we found a pearl?
The divers do.
One by one they go
over the mossy side and disappear,
stowing what breath they can about the heart.

They rock the boat. We wait
uneasily to count returning heads,
feeling under the sky
their airlessness,
the pressure in their ears.

How long and deep they've gone
taking our perishable atmosphere
under the bay, into a country mapped
with nerves, inhabited by darting eyes
in coral tenements, irritable shells.

Do the natives watch them,
do they come expected
so the doors are bolted, what
to the evanescent fish
are those brown slender creatures

diamonded about the face with air?
They dive for the pearl beds.
Otherworldly, purposeful, they seem
angel visitors. With knives
they choose and crack a likely shell,

pick out the pearl and place it in their mouths
then climb out of the water's sky.
Some angels fail and settle and are eaten.
The coral anchors them.
They turn to stone.

What would we do if we were angels there —
be resolutely blind to the exotic
citizens, the stings, the shadows,
nose out the oyster's neighbourhood,
hold our knife to its blunt lips

like surgery or love, and cut
the tongue to free the precious word?
Could we crawl up the water then,
taking the weight of what we did
out through the mirror to our element?

What would we have to sell?
— The broken mouths would call;
the weeds send subtle arms
after like tendrils and settle us;
cupped in our cheeks the pearls

last longer, though they are less white, than bone.
If we would be angels
we should find only a world
we leave untouched will suffer us.
And if its shells

gape to tempt us,
beneath their iridescent tongues
we recognize a bribe for other lips.
We husband our breath only and bring home
nothing, and cause nothing, and are free.

THE SHELLS
(a guided tour in the Andes)

These shells are from no familiar sea —
they litter furrows in the mountain fields.
Ploughing turns them over year to year.
They come back more predictably than maize:

almost ordinary, like a worker's bruised nails,
but inside luminous in certain lights
as mother pearl. They are stone now. The plough
can chip them but they are the years':

they do not break outright.
When these mountains were lifted from the sea
they carried the live cities of the sea —
the scallop beds, the clams in families

fisted on to marl, and sand a pure
salt white. The water rilled away; the salts
have worked their passage back to water.
The shells stayed until they are these stones

among farmers who have never seen the sea
or tasted fish, who plough with wood
and weed by hand and touch them as elaborate
queer flints or coloured stones.

This is what time does when history
leaves it to itself — retrieves organic
monuments for a longer eternity than ours —
these mute informers that are twice over

stone: of memory and stone. We might
stop here a day and gather them
as Darwin did in sacks, to ship home
for minute interrogation. We might spend

an hour with the Indian farmers
to whom we are enigmas, rich and pale,
and tell them how the fine-lipped shells,
the delicate bright eyes of soil are not

real stone, how these coarse fields
plunder a dead sea city that —
if they knew its language —
could rob them of their given catechism.

Better leave them be, each to his field,
ploughing securely towards their seventh day.
We have our own sufficient luggage
of broken promises and curios for home.

The bus is waiting and our tribe is tired.
We'll keep a secret they could not believe
and let the shells be turned and turned for seasons
as the unspent coins of passage out of faith.

THE FREEZE

We can't sleep tonight. The ice has formed —
from thin skin at evening
to deep stone. With midnight
the boat's aground in it.
Planks shriek against the hardening.

Below deck a film of frost pales everything.
Our breath makes beads of ice. We pace
between the hatch and bunks.
The world would end by ice
tonight, for sure, if we lay down.

Come outside: the wind has sculpted
sails to marble drapery;
on the line our laundry freezes to
a rigor-mortis of our bodies' clothes.
Night will hardly darken all this glass —

the stars are treble on its rippled plane.
Birds stiffen on the surface,
bellies up, like fish.
We started from a tropic on whose shore
the lizards' tongues were flames of malachite

in leaves that trailed on to the tide,
and crimson fish were couriers there
to caverns where eels uncoiled their sting.
Night plankton burned our wake —
for years we have been heading north.

When lips are tucked away for good
and rigid as ice-starched shirt and trousers
we pass the climax of our slow miasma,
and the river hardens in the arteries
till the heart with the hull surrenders

to stillness and is broken like a stone,
when our histories are minuted, adjourned,
our faces upturned to a Sabbath star,
this will be the scene if we can see,
the fish arrested with the drifting tyres,

the dry snow driven into dunes of ash.
It was not like this in the other place —
there all was fire and water,
nothing stilled the waves
that might be furious though they never died

to the intolerable vacancy
we pace to keep the blood awake. Come down.
We'll light the burner, thaw our fingers out.
We are the ashes that will cover us,
our inch of life, our mile, our field of breathing.

THE DIVING BELL

They slam the hatch. Sealed
in a mutual air we are raised up.
The steel arm swings us out.
The cable sings.
Like some hard bait we are released

and plunge, a bubble weightier
than sea water, fathoming in spirals
the currents of sea light.
We are like the pendant world
the tempter saw, except

it is not a gold chain that fastens us
and no god lets us down
bright steps and shafts into
the water's evening, towards a night
we were not meant to penetrate.

What is it about depth
attracts us and we go
further than day can into the sea,
beyond the dwindling colour of known fish
into a region of eyes that gaze

through ebony? Our bell falls
more gently into dark than light,
reaching seabed. It rolls on its side.
Should the cable break now we are home
here as in Hell.

We sit still.
We peer into a total pitch
that slowly lives. Bright things
bearing their own light advance
their futureless star eyes

to the rim of our portholes. Their lips
with uninvented voices kiss the panes.
We taste of air.
We light the lamps
and cause along the beds of furred shale

births, approaching us like crippled birds:
livid, rippling tissue wings, and diffident
swallow fish we feed with light:
as though we were St Francis's hand
reached out to raise up a forsaken tribe

our five lamps feel each way
and, touching, blind.
Under tons of water the fish bear
all movement in a gradual agony.
This is the depth from which death raises them.

Colour that never was before
glows with a crude, wounded brilliance.
We do not know these creatures:
pressure distorts theirs to a dayless world
with no history but the living

relics that find motion
the way dream-creatures do —
they do not measure time
and if they touch sharp stone,
or sometimes when they mate,

they burst, a scattering cloud
in their lost atmosphere.
We rest upon their bed.
We are awake here, naming —
as Darwin did in the unknown fossil worlds

that live in us, or Dante
from the pit, carrying his shadow
where we would be eternal in the maze.
We will be drawn up from this world
with only words to show — but they are true;

each coast we tried before
was wrong, until we left the map
into untaken courses.
We will go home and sketch
a chart we know is real and unbelievable.